SEASHELLS OF GEORGIA AND THE CAROLINAS UPDATED EDITION

A Smart Beachcomber's Lead

Rae M. Clive

TABLE OF CONTENTS

CHAPTER THREE

Seashells of the Carolinas

Coastal Habitats of the Carolinas

INTRODUCTION

Settled within the gentle ebb and flow of the Atlantic Ocean lie the coastal treasures of Georgia and the Carolinas, where the shorelines whisper tales of natural beauty and timeless allure. None of the myriad gifts bestowed by these pristine waters captivates the imagination quite like the seashell. Symbolic of the sea's artistry and the intricate rhythms of marine life, seashells have long enchanted beachcombers, scientists, and collectors alike with their stunning diversity and fascinating stories.

In this meticulously updated edition of "Seashells of Georgia and the Carolinas," we embark on a journey to unravel the secrets of these coastal gems. Every page unveils a mosaic of shapes, colors, and textures, each shell a testament to the rich biodiversity and ecological richness of the Southeastern seaboard. From the windswept dunes of Georgia's barrier islands to the tidal flats of the Outer Banks and beyond, this guide is a celebration of the region's unparalleled seashell diversity.

Expertly curated and lavishly illustrated, this edition blends scientific rigor with the wonder of discovery. It serves as a comprehensive resource for enthusiasts, researchers, and casual beachgoers alike, offering detailed descriptions, vivid photographs, and insightful commentary on hundreds of species. Whether you seek to identify a newfound treasure washed ashore or simply wish to deepen your appreciation for the natural world, this book promises to be your trusted companion.

Beyond its role as a field guide, "Seashells of Georgia and the Carolinas" beckons us to contemplate the broader narrative of our planet's interconnected ecosystems. Each shell tells a tale of adaptation, survival, and the delicate balance of life beneath the waves. As our understanding of climate change and environmental stewardship evolves, these coastal habitats and their inhabitants remind us of the urgent need for conservation and preservation.

With its blend of scientific expertise and passion for natural beauty, this updated edition stands as a testament to the enduring allure of seashells and the profound importance of safeguarding our coastal treasures for future generations. Join us on a voyage of discovery along the shores of Georgia and the Carolinas, where every shell holds a story waiting to be told, and where the beauty of the sea meets the curiosity of the human spirit.

CHAPTER ONE

Introduction to Seashells

What are Seashells?

Seashells, those exquisite treasures of the shorelines, evoke wonder and fascination in both children and adults alike. Beyond their aesthetic appeal, seashells hold a wealth of biological, ecological, and cultural significance. Let's delve into the intricacies of seashells to uncover their mysteries.

Anatomy and Formation

Seashells are the protective outer coverings of marine mollusks, a diverse group of invertebrate animals belonging to the phylum Mollusca. Mollusks encompass a wide range of species, including snails, clams, oysters, and octopuses, but it is primarily the gastropods and bivalves that produce the majority of seashells.

Gastropod Shells: These are typically spiral-shaped, formed as the mollusk secretes calcium carbonate to create a series of chambers as it grows. The intricate patterns and shapes vary widely among species, reflecting adaptations to their environments.

Bivalve Shells: Characterized by two hinged halves (valves), bivalve shells like those of clams and oysters are usually symmetrical. They are formed when the mollusk secretes calcium carbonate that solidifies into the shell structure.

Composition and Structure

Seashells are composed primarily of calcium carbonate ($CaCO_3$), which is deposited in layers by the mollusk's mantle, a specialized tissue responsible for shell formation. The structure of the shell includes:

Outer Layer: Known as the periostracum, this layer is often thin, tough, and composed of organic compounds such as conchiolin, which gives some shells their glossy appearance.

Middle Layer: The prismatic layer, consisting of densely packed calcium carbonate crystals arranged in a matrix. This layer provides strength and structural integrity to the shell.

Inner Layer: The nacreous layer, also called mother-of-pearl, is made up of thin layers of calcium carbonate crystals. It gives some shells their iridescent sheen and is highly valued for decorative purposes.

Ecological Importance

Seashells play crucial roles in marine ecosystems:

Habitat and Protection: Many marine organisms use empty shells for shelter and protection from predators, contributing to biodiversity and ecological balance.

Calcium Source: Calcium from shells can dissolve into seawater, replenishing this essential nutrient for other marine organisms like corals and algae.

Cultural Significance

Throughout history and across cultures, seashells have held symbolic and practical value:

Art and Decoration: Seashells have been used for millennia as decorative items, jewelry, and art objects. They feature prominently in indigenous cultures and coastal communities worldwide.

Symbolism: Seashells often symbolize themes such as fertility, birth, and the ocean's bounty. They appear in myths, folklore, and religious ceremonies globally.

Human Interaction

Humans have long interacted with seashells in various ways:

Collection: Seashell collecting, or conchology, is a popular hobby and scientific pursuit, driving exploration and research into marine biodiversity.

Economic Use: Historically, shells have been harvested for their calcium carbonate content, used in lime production, and even ground into fine powders for use in cosmetics and pharmaceuticals.

Conservation and Sustainability

Given their cultural, ecological, and economic significance, the conservation of seashell habitats and species is crucial. Practices such as sustainable harvesting, habitat protection, and public awareness are essential to ensure the longevity and diversity of seashells for future generations.

Seashells are not just objects washed ashore; they are intricate products of nature's ingenuity, embodying centuries of natural history and cultural heritage. Their beauty and complexity continue to inspire scientists, artists, and beachcombers worldwide, highlighting the interconnectedness of marine life and human civilization. As we appreciate seashells, let us also strive to protect the fragile ecosystems that nurture these marvels of the sea.

Importance of Seashells in Coastal Ecosystems
Seashells, often admired for their beauty and diversity, play crucial roles in coastal ecosystems beyond their aesthetic appeal. These calcium carbonate structures, formed by marine mollusks, contribute significantly to the health and balance of coastal environments worldwide. Here's an in-depth exploration of their multifaceted importance:

1. Habitat and Shelter
Seashells provide essential habitats and shelter for numerous marine organisms. Small fish, crabs, and other invertebrates seek refuge within empty shells, utilizing them as protective cover from predators and

harsh environmental conditions. In this way, seashells enhance biodiversity by offering safe havens that support the entire food web.

2. Nutrient Cycling

As seashells decompose, they release calcium carbonate into the surrounding environment. This process helps buffer pH levels and maintain the alkalinity of seawater, which is crucial for the health of marine organisms like corals and shellfish. Additionally, the breakdown of seashells releases essential nutrients such as calcium and carbon into the ecosystem, which are utilized by various organisms for growth and development.

3. Erosion Control

Seashells contribute to coastal stability by forming natural barriers and substrates. They can accumulate in intertidal zones and along shorelines, helping to dissipate wave energy and reduce erosion. Coastal areas with abundant seashells often experience less erosion compared to those without, demonstrating their role in maintaining the integrity of coastal landscapes.

4. Ecological Interactions

The presence of seashells influences ecological interactions in coastal ecosystems. They serve as attachment surfaces for algae and other organisms, contributing to the formation of complex microhabitats that foster diverse communities. These interactions are vital for nutrient cycling and energy transfer within marine ecosystems, ultimately supporting the productivity and resilience of coastal habitats.

5. Indicator of Environmental Health

The condition and distribution of seashells can serve as indicators of environmental health and ecological changes. Changes in shell morphology, species distribution, or shell density may reflect shifts in environmental conditions such as temperature, pH levels, or pollution levels. Monitoring seashell populations can provide valuable insights into the overall health of coastal ecosystems and the impacts of human activities.

6. Cultural and Economic Importance

Seashells hold cultural significance in many coastal communities worldwide. They have been used historically for crafting jewelry, ornaments, and tools, contributing to local economies through tourism and artisanal activities. Understanding the ecological importance of seashells can enhance conservation efforts and sustainable practices that benefit both ecosystems and human communities.

7. Research and Conservation

Seashells are valuable subjects of scientific research, offering insights into evolutionary biology, ecology, and paleontology. Studying shell structures and compositions can reveal information about past climates, species adaptations, and ecosystem dynamics. Conservation efforts focused on protecting seashell habitats are crucial for maintaining biodiversity and preserving the ecological services they provide.

In conclusion, seashells are not merely decorative objects found on beaches; they are integral components of coastal ecosystems with profound ecological, cultural, and economic importance.

Recognizing and protecting the roles that seashells play can contribute to the sustainable management and conservation of coastal environments for future generations.

Historical and Cultural Significance of Seashells
Seashells have captivated human imagination and culture for millennia, transcending their humble origins as remnants of marine life. Their historical and cultural significance spans across civilizations, continents, and centuries, weaving a tapestry of symbolism, practicality, and artistic expression.

1. Symbolism and Spiritual Significance
Seashells have often been imbued with spiritual meanings across various cultures:

Ancient Cultures: In ancient Greece, seashells were associated with Aphrodite, the goddess of love and beauty, symbolizing fertility and femininity. They were also used as offerings to the gods.

Native American Traditions: Many Native American tribes, such as the Hopi and Navajo, used shells in ceremonies and rituals. The shells were believed to have protective powers and were worn as amulets.

Asian Cultures: In Japan, shells were considered symbols of good fortune and were used in traditional art forms like netsuke and inlaid lacquerware.

2. Practical Uses in History

Beyond symbolism, seashells served practical purposes throughout history:

Currency and Trade: Certain types of shells, such as cowries, were used as currency in various parts of the world, including Africa, Asia, and Oceania. They facilitated trade and commerce long before the advent of coins.

Tools and Ornaments: Early humans used seashells as tools, such as cutting implements or containers for food and water. They were also crafted into jewelry and decorative objects.

3. Artistic Expression
Seashells have inspired artists and artisans across different cultures:

Mosaic Art: In ancient Rome and Byzantium, seashells were used in intricate mosaic designs, decorating floors and walls of important buildings like temples and palaces.

Decorative Arts: In Victorian England, the fascination with shells led to the creation of "shellwork" or "sailor's valentines," intricate designs made from shells, which sailors brought back from their voyages as gifts.

4. Scientific and Environmental Significance

Seashells also hold scientific importance:

Study of Biodiversity: Marine biologists and ecologists study shells to understand biodiversity, ecological health, and evolutionary history of marine organisms.

Environmental Indicators: Changes in shell characteristics, such as thickness or shape, can indicate environmental changes like pollution or climate change.

5. Modern–Day Relevance and Conservation

Today, seashells continue to be cherished for their beauty and cultural significance:

Tourism and Souvenirs: Coastal communities worldwide rely on seashells as tourist attractions and souvenirs, contributing to local economies.

Conservation Efforts: Due to over-harvesting and habitat destruction, many species of shell-bearing organisms are threatened. Conservation efforts aim to protect these species and their habitats.

In conclusion, seashells are not just remnants of marine life; they are repositories of history, culture, and natural beauty. From ancient spiritual practices to modern-day conservation efforts, their significance transcends time and borders, reminding us of our deep and enduring connection to the ocean and its diverse ecosystems. As we navigate the complexities of the modern world, understanding and preserving the historical and cultural significance of seashells remains paramount.

Overview of Seashell Classification

Seashells have fascinated humans for centuries, not just for their aesthetic appeal but also for their diversity and the insights they provide into marine ecosystems. The classification of seashells is a complex field that combines elements of biology, taxonomy, and natural history. Here's a detailed overview of how seashells are classified, the key characteristics used in their classification, and the importance of understanding their diversity.

Importance of Seashell Classification

Seashells serve as protective outer coverings for mollusks, such as snails, clams, and cephalopods, and play crucial roles in their survival and reproduction. Understanding seashell classification helps scientists:

Identify Species: Different species of mollusks can often be identified by their unique shell characteristics, aiding in species conservation and management.

Study Evolution: Seashells provide valuable clues about the evolutionary history of mollusks and their adaptations to different environments over millions of years.

Monitor Ecosystems: Changes in seashell populations can indicate shifts in marine ecosystems, making them important indicators for environmental monitoring.

Principles of Seashell Classification

Seashell classification follows a hierarchical system based on observable traits. These traits include:

Shell Shape: Seashells exhibit a remarkable variety of shapes, from spiral to conical, globular, and bivalve (two-piece). The shape often correlates with the lifestyle and habitat of the mollusk.

Shell Size: Size ranges from tiny microshells to large specimens like the giant clam. Size can also be an indicator of maturity and environmental factors.

Surface Sculpture: The texture and ornamentation on the shell's surface, such as ribs, spines, or grooves, are important for classification.

Aperture Characteristics: The opening of the shell (aperture) varies greatly among species and can be round, elongated, or have specialized structures like siphonal canals.

Color and Pattern: Shell coloration can vary widely and may serve functions such as camouflage, species recognition, or protection from UV radiation.

Classification Systems

Seashell classification employs several taxonomic systems, with the most common being:

Linnaean Taxonomy: Classifies shells into hierarchical categories such as kingdom, phylum, class, order, family, genus, and species based on anatomical and morphological features.

Conchology: The study of shells, focusing on their classification, morphology, ecology, and evolution.

Morphometrics: Uses quantitative measurements of shell characteristics for statistical analysis, aiding in species differentiation and phylogenetic studies.

Major Shell Types

Seashells are broadly categorized based on the structure and symmetry of their shells:

Gastropods: Univalve shells (e.g., snails) characterized by a single, spiraling shell.

Bivalves: Two-piece shells (e.g., clams) hinged along one edge, typically symmetrical.

Cephalopods: Internal shells (e.g., squid, octopus) or absent shells (e.g., nautilus), adapted for fast movement and predation.

Challenges and Future Directions

Classifying seashells faces challenges due to factors such as shell variability within species, convergent evolution, and limited availability of taxonomic experts. However, advancements in imaging technology and genetic analysis are aiding in more accurate and comprehensive classifications.

Seashell classification is not merely an academic pursuit but a vital tool for understanding marine biodiversity, evolution, and ecosystem health. By studying seashells, scientists gain insights into the natural history of mollusks and their habitats, paving the way for informed conservation efforts and a deeper appreciation of the wonders of the ocean.

In summary, the classification of seashells combines art and science, offering a glimpse into the intricate world of marine life and the profound interplay between form, function, and environment.

Tools and Techniques for Seashell Collection
Seashell collection, or conchology, is a fascinating hobby that allows enthusiasts to explore the beauty and diversity of shells found along coastlines worldwide. Whether you're a beginner or a seasoned collector, having the right tools and techniques can enhance your experience and help you build a stunning collection. Here's a comprehensive guide to tools and techniques for seashell collection:

Tools for Seashell Collection:

Mesh Bags or Buckets: These are essential for carrying your finds without damaging delicate shells. Mesh bags allow sand and water to drain, keeping your shells in good condition.

Trowel or Small Shovel: Useful for digging in sandy or muddy areas where shells might be partially buried.

Waterproof Gloves: Protect your hands from sharp edges and ensure a good grip, especially when handling live shells.

Small Brush: A soft-bristled brush like a paintbrush helps gently remove sand and debris from shells without causing damage.

Magnifying Glass: Useful for examining small details and identifying tiny shells or intricate patterns.

Shell Identification Guide: A book or a reliable mobile app can help you identify shells based on their characteristics such as shape, color, and patterns.

Camera: Capture high-quality images of your shells, especially if you plan to document or share your collection.

Measuring Tape or Caliper: Useful for recording the size of shells accurately, which can aid in identification and documentation.

Pliers or Tweezers: Helpful for extracting shells from tight spaces or crevices without damaging them.

Diving Mask and Snorkel (optional): If collecting in shallow waters, these can enhance your ability to spot shells and explore underwater habitats.

Techniques for Seashell Collection:

Respect Local Regulations: Ensure you are allowed to collect shells in the area you are visiting. Some places have restrictions to protect marine habitats.

Time and Tide: Visit beaches at low tide for the best chance of finding shells that are exposed by receding waters. Early morning often yields the freshest finds before they are picked over.

Search Diverse Habitats: Shells can be found on sandy beaches, rocky shores, in tidal pools, and even buried in mud. Explore different environments for a variety of species.

Handle with Care: Many shells are fragile. Avoid picking up live specimens or damaging shells you don't intend to collect. Replace live shells gently back into their natural habitat.

Clean and Preserve: Rinse shells with fresh water to remove sand and debris. For long–term preservation, soak shells briefly in a diluted bleach solution to sanitize and brighten them, then rinse thoroughly and air dry.

Document Your Collection: Record where and when each shell was found, along with any observations about its condition or habitat. This adds value to your collection and aids in identification.

Learn and Share: Join local shell clubs or online communities to learn more about shells, share your finds, and connect with other enthusiasts.

Ethical Collection: Avoid over-collecting rare or endangered species. Respect conservation efforts and leave shells in their natural habitats when appropriate.

Storage: Store shells in a dry, cool place away from direct sunlight to prevent fading or deterioration. Display them in shadow boxes or glass cases to protect them from dust and damage.

Continuous Learning: Expand your knowledge of shells by reading books, attending workshops, or participating in field trips led by experts.

The Seashell collection is not just a hobby but a way to appreciate the intricate beauty and diversity of marine life. By using the right tools and techniques, you can enhance your collection while contributing to the conservation of coastal ecosystems. Enjoy the thrill of discovery and the satisfaction of building a unique and meaningful collection of seashells!

CHAPTER TWO

Seashells of Georgia

Coastal Habitats of Georgia

Georgia's coastal habitats are diverse and ecologically rich environments that play a crucial role in supporting a wide array of flora, fauna, and human activities. From salt marshes to barrier islands, each habitat type contributes uniquely to the overall biodiversity and ecological health of the region. Here, we delve into the various coastal habitats of Georgia, their significance, the threats they face, and conservation efforts aimed at preserving these invaluable ecosystems.

1. Salt Marshes:

Salt marshes are one of the most vital coastal habitats in Georgia, characterized by their unique blend of salt-tolerant plants and dynamic tidal cycles. These marshes act as natural buffers against storm surges, filter pollutants, and provide nurseries for numerous marine species, including shrimp, crabs, and fish. The Georgia coast boasts extensive salt marshes, such as the expansive marshes of the Altamaha River delta and the lush estuarine ecosystems of Cumberland Island.

Conservation Challenges: Salt marshes are vulnerable to habitat loss due to coastal development, sea-level rise, and invasive species. Efforts to protect these habitats include land-use planning, restoration projects, and monitoring of water quality.

2. Barrier Islands:

Georgia's barrier islands form a protective barrier between the mainland and the Atlantic Ocean, serving as natural defenses against hurricanes and storms. These islands are characterized by their dunes, maritime forests, and beaches, which provide critical nesting sites for seabirds, sea turtles, and other wildlife.

Conservation Challenges: Barrier islands face threats from erosion, rising sea levels, and human activities such as development, which can disrupt natural processes and habitats. Conservation efforts include dune restoration, beach nourishment projects, and restrictions on coastal construction.

3. Estuaries:

Estuaries are where freshwater rivers meet the salty ocean, creating a unique blend of habitats that support a diverse range of marine and terrestrial species. Georgia's estuaries, such as those along the Savannah and Altamaha Rivers, are essential for commercial fisheries, recreational activities, and as feeding grounds for migratory birds.

Conservation Challenges: Estuaries are vulnerable to pollution from runoff, habitat degradation, and overfishing. Conservation strategies focus on watershed management, habitat restoration, and sustainable fishing practices to maintain ecological balance.

4. Coral Reefs:

While not as extensive as those found in tropical regions, Georgia's offshore reefs are important for biodiversity, supporting various species of corals, sponges, and fish. These reefs provide essential habitat and serve as breeding grounds for commercially   important   fish   species.

Conservation Challenges: Coral reefs are threatened by warming waters, ocean acidification, and physical damage from human activities such as anchoring and fishing. Conservation efforts include marine protected areas, coral restoration initiatives, and monitoring programs to assess reef health.

5. Mangrove Forests:

Mangrove forests, found primarily in the southernmost coastal regions of Georgia, are salt-tolerant trees and shrubs that stabilize shorelines, provide nurseries for fish and crustaceans, and filter pollutants from coastal waters.

Conservation Challenges: Mangrove forests face threats from coastal development, habitat destruction, and climate change impacts like sea-level rise and storms. Conservation measures include mangrove restoration projects, protected areas designation, and community engagement in coastal stewardship.

Conservation Efforts:

Conservation organizations, government agencies, and local communities in Georgia are actively engaged in protecting and preserving these vital coastal habitats. Key conservation efforts include:

Habitat Restoration: Projects aimed at restoring degraded habitats such as salt marshes, dunes, and oyster reefs.

Research and Monitoring: Long-term studies to understand ecosystem dynamics, biodiversity trends, and the impacts of climate change.

Education and Outreach: Public awareness campaigns to promote conservation ethics, sustainable practices, and the importance of coastal ecosystems.

Policy and Regulation: Implementation of regulations and zoning laws to mitigate coastal development impacts and ensure sustainable resource management.

Georgia's coastal habitats are not only ecologically significant but also economically and culturally important to the region. Sustaining these habitats requires concerted efforts from government agencies, conservation organizations, and local communities to address current challenges and prepare for future environmental changes. By understanding the complexities of these ecosystems and implementing effective conservation strategies, we can ensure the long–term health and resilience of Georgia's coastal habitats for generations to come.

Common Seashell Species in Georgia
Lightning Whelk (Sinistrofulgur perversum)

The Lightning Whelk, scientifically known as Sinistrofulgur perversum, is a striking mollusk found along the southeastern coast of the United States, including the shores of Georgia. Known for its distinct spiral shell and predatory habits, this species holds ecological significance and captivates beachcombers and researchers alike with its unique characteristics.

Physical Description

The Lightning Whelk is easily recognizable by its large, spiraling shell which typically grows up to 16 inches in length, making it one of the largest whelks in North America. The shell exhibits a creamy white to grayish background color adorned with irregular reddish–brown streaks or spots resembling lightning bolts, hence its common name. Unlike most gastropods that coil to the right, the Lightning

Whelk's shell is sinistral, coiling to the left, which is rare among marine snails.

Distribution and Habitat

In Georgia, Lightning Whelks are commonly found in the shallow coastal waters of the Atlantic Ocean and along the intertidal zones of barrier islands. They prefer sandy or muddy substrates where they can bury themselves partially and wait for their prey. These whelks are also known to inhabit estuaries and marshes, where they play a crucial role in the local marine ecosystem.

Behavior and Feeding Habits

As carnivorous predators, Lightning Whelks feed primarily on bivalve mollusks such as clams and oysters. Using their muscular foot, they pry open the shells of their prey and then use a radula (a toothed tongue–like organ) to scrape and consume the soft tissues inside. Their feeding habits contribute to controlling populations of bivalves, which helps maintain the balance within coastal ecosystems.

Reproduction and Life Cycle

During the breeding season, which typically occurs in spring and summer, Lightning Whelks engage in internal fertilization. Females lay egg capsules that contain numerous small, developing whelks. These egg capsules are often found washed up on beaches and are commonly referred to as "mermaid's purses." The larvae hatch and undergo a planktonic stage before settling on the seafloor as juvenile whelks.

Ecological Importance

Lightning Whelks play a vital role in Georgia's coastal ecosystems. By preying on bivalve populations, they help regulate these species' numbers, preventing overpopulation that could have detrimental effects on local habitats. Additionally, their shells provide a habitat for smaller organisms and contribute to the overall biodiversity of the coastal environment.

Conservation Status and Threats

While not currently listed as threatened or endangered, Lightning Whelks face potential threats from habitat loss due to coastal development, pollution, and climate change. Efforts to monitor populations and protect their habitats are essential for ensuring the continued presence of these fascinating creatures along Georgia's coastline.

Human Interaction and Uses

Throughout history, Lightning Whelks have been utilized by humans for various purposes. Indigenous peoples and early settlers used their shells for tools, adornments, and even ceremonial purposes. Today, these shells are sought after by collectors and artisans for their aesthetic appeal and cultural significance, contributing to local economies through tourism and artisanal crafts.

The Lightning Whelk, Sinistrofulgur perversum, stands out not only for its distinctive appearance and predatory nature but also for its ecological importance along the coast of Georgia. As a keystone species in its habitat, this mollusk symbolizes the delicate balance of marine ecosystems and serves as a reminder of the interconnectedness between land, sea, and human activities.

Understanding and appreciating the Lightning Whelk not only enriches our knowledge of marine biodiversity but also underscores the importance of conservation efforts to ensure the preservation of these remarkable creatures for future generations.

Calico Scallop (Argopecten gibbus)

The Calico Scallop, scientifically known as Argopecten gibbus, is a fascinating and commonly found seashell species along the coastal waters of Georgia. This bivalve mollusk belongs to the family Pectinidae and is renowned for its striking appearance and ecological significance in the region.

Physical Characteristics

The Calico Scallop exhibits a distinctive shell that typically measures between 5 to 8 centimeters in diameter, though larger specimens can occasionally be found. Its shell is convex and fairly smooth, adorned with intricate radial ribs that radiate from the hinge area. These ribs are often colored in shades of orange, red, brown, and sometimes purple, giving rise to its common name "Calico" due to the resemblance to colorful patchwork fabric. The interior of the shell is glossy and varies from white to a deep, pearly purple.

Habitat and Distribution

This species thrives in shallow coastal waters, particularly in sandy or muddy substrates where it can bury itself just beneath the surface. Along the Georgia coastline, from Cumberland Island to the southern border with Florida, the Calico Scallop is abundant. It prefers waters with moderate salinity levels and can often be found in intertidal zones or in depths of up to 30 meters.

Feeding and Ecology

As a filter feeder, Argopecten gibbus plays a crucial role in its ecosystem by consuming plankton and organic particles suspended in the water. Its method of feeding involves pumping water through its gills and extracting food particles, which not only sustains the scallop but also helps in maintaining water clarity and quality.

Reproduction and Life Cycle

Calico Scallops are dioecious, meaning individuals are either male or female. Reproduction typically occurs during the warmer months when water temperatures are favorable. Fertilization occurs externally, and the larvae, known as veligers, undergo a period of free–swimming before settling onto suitable substrates to undergo metamorphosis into juvenile scallops. This process is vital for maintaining populations and ensuring genetic diversity within the species.

Economic and Cultural Importance

Beyond its ecological role, the Calico Scallop holds economic significance in Georgia. While not as commercially harvested as some larger scallop species, it contributes to the biodiversity of local marine environments and supports recreational shellfish harvesting activities. The scallop's attractive shell also makes it a sought–after item for collectors and beachcombers, contributing to local tourism and cultural appreciation of marine life.

Conservation Status and Threats

Like many marine species, the Calico Scallop faces threats from habitat degradation, pollution, and climate change. Efforts to monitor populations and protect critical habitats are crucial for ensuring its continued presence along the Georgia coastline. Conservation initiatives aimed at sustainable management of coastal resources play a pivotal role in safeguarding not only Argopecten gibbus but also the broader marine ecosystems it inhabits.

In conclusion, the Calico Scallop (Argopecten gibbus) stands as a symbol of the rich biodiversity found along Georgia's coastal waters. Its colorful shell, ecological role as a filter feeder, and economic value highlight its importance both environmentally and culturally. By understanding and protecting this species, we contribute to the preservation of Georgia's marine heritage for future generations to appreciate and enjoy.

Lettered Olive (Oliva sayana)
The Lettered Olive (Oliva sayana) stands as a distinctive and abundant species of seashell found along the coast of Georgia, enriching the region's diverse marine ecosystem. Renowned for its unique characteristics and ecological significance, the

Lettered Olive captivates both scientists and beachcombers alike.

Physical Characteristics

The Lettered Olive shell is renowned for its elongated shape, typically reaching lengths of 1.5 to 3 inches. Its smooth surface is marked by a glossy, pale beige color, occasionally tinted with shades of pink or yellow. What truly sets the Lettered Olive apart are the intricate markings that adorn its shell: fine, raised lines that spiral around its length, resembling delicate calligraphy, hence its name.

Habitat and Distribution

Oliva sayana thrives in the shallow coastal waters and sandy shores of Georgia. These shells often wash ashore in large numbers, especially after storms, making them a common find for beachcombers along the state's barrier islands and mainland beaches. Their distribution extends from the Gulf of Mexico to the Atlantic coast, with Georgia being a notable hotspot due to its favorable coastal conditions.

Ecological Importance

Beyond their aesthetic appeal, Lettered Olives play crucial ecological roles. They serve as habitats and protective covers for various marine organisms during their lifecycle. Additionally, their presence influences sediment dynamics and nutrient cycling in coastal environments, contributing to the overall health of local ecosystems.

Cultural and Recreational Significance

The Lettered Olive holds cultural significance as well, often featured in local arts and crafts and historically used by indigenous peoples for ornamentation. Today, they remain popular among collectors and enthusiasts who appreciate their beauty and intricate patterns. For beachgoers, finding a pristine Lettered Olive shell is a cherished experience, symbolizing the natural beauty and diversity of Georgia's coastline.

Conservation and Management

While not currently listed as endangered, monitoring and conservation efforts are essential to maintain healthy populations of Oliva sayana. Coastal development and climate change pose potential threats to their habitat, emphasizing the need for sustainable coastal management practices and awareness among local communities and visitors.

In conclusion, the Lettered Olive (Oliva sayana) stands as a quintessential symbol of Georgia's coastal biodiversity. Its elegant form, coupled with its ecological and cultural significance, makes it a beloved icon among seashell enthusiasts and conservationists alike. By understanding and appreciating the role of the Lettered Olive in Georgia's marine environment, we can ensure its presence for generations to come, fostering a deeper connection between humans and the natural world.

Whether strolling along Georgia's beaches or exploring its vibrant marine life, the Lettered Olive serves as a reminder of the intricate beauty and ecological richness found along the southeastern coast of the United States.

Knobbed Whelk (Busycon carica)

The Knobbed Whelk, scientifically known as Busycon carica, stands as a prominent and recognizable seashell species inhabiting the coastal waters of Georgia. Renowned for its robust shell and distinctive spiral structure, this marine gastropod mollusk holds significant ecological and cultural importance in the region.

Physical Characteristics

The shell of the Knobbed Whelk is characterized by its large size and intricate design. Typically, it features a conical shape with a prominent spire and a series of rounded knobs spiraling along its length. These knobs serve not only as aesthetic features but also as protective elements, helping deter predators from attacking the mollusk within.

Coloration varies widely, ranging from shades of light tan to darker brown, often blending with the sandy or muddy substrates where they are commonly found. The inner surface of the shell is typically smooth and glossy, contrasting with the outer textured appearance.

Distribution and Habitat

Busycon carica thrives in the shallow coastal waters of Georgia, favoring sandy or muddy substrates where it can bury itself partially to hunt for prey such as bivalves and crustaceans. It is also known to inhabit seagrass beds and oyster reefs, where it plays a crucial role in the marine ecosystem by controlling populations of its prey species.

These whelks are most commonly found from the intertidal zone down to depths of around 50 feet, although occasional specimens can be found deeper. Their distribution extends along the Atlantic coast of

North America, from Massachusetts to the Gulf of Mexico, with notable populations residing in the warm waters of Georgia's coast.

Ecological Role

As a predator, the Knobbed Whelk helps maintain balance within coastal ecosystems by feeding on other mollusks and invertebrates. This role makes it an important factor in the health of oyster populations and the overall biodiversity of the region. Furthermore, the shells of deceased whelks provide a habitat for small marine organisms, contributing to the complex web of life in the coastal environment.

Cultural Significance

Beyond its ecological role, the Knobbed Whelk holds cultural significance among coastal communities in Georgia. Historically, Native American tribes used whelk shells for various purposes, including as tools, ornaments, and ceremonial items. Today, these shells continue to be prized for their beauty and are often collected by beachcombers and shell enthusiasts.

Conservation Status and Management

While not currently listed as endangered, the Knobbed Whelk faces threats from habitat degradation, pollution, and overharvesting. In Georgia, conservation efforts focus on sustainable harvesting practices and monitoring of wild populations to ensure their long-term viability. Regulations are in place to limit the collection of live specimens and protect critical habitats where these whelks reside.

In conclusion, the Knobbed Whelk (Busycon carica) stands as a symbol of the rich biodiversity and cultural heritage of Georgia's coastal regions. From its striking shell design to its essential ecological role, this species continues to fascinate scientists, conservationists, and beachgoers alike. Preserving the habitat and populations of the Knobbed Whelk ensures that future generations can continue to appreciate its beauty and importance in our natural world.

Coquina (Donax variabilis)

Coquina, scientifically known as Donax variabilis, is a small bivalve mollusk commonly found along the shores of Georgia, particularly in the southeastern United States. Known for its vibrant array of colors and unique ecological adaptations, coquina shells play a significant role in coastal ecosystems and human history alike.

Physical Characteristics

Coquina shells are relatively small, typically measuring between 0.5 to 1 inch in length. They are wedge-shaped and feature symmetrical, rounded ends. The shells are characterized by a range of colors, including white, pink, yellow, and purple, often forming striking patterns and variations within populations. This variability in coloration gives rise to their species name, variabilis, which means variable.

Habitat and Distribution

Coquinas inhabit sandy beaches and shallow coastal waters, where they burrow into the substrate to feed on plankton and organic detritus. They are particularly abundant in intertidal zones, where the water level fluctuates with the tides. Along the coast of Georgia, coquinas can be found from the barrier islands to the mainland beaches, thriving in the sandy bottoms where they are well-camouflaged against predators like shorebirds and fish.

Ecological Significance

Filter Feeders: Coquinas play a crucial ecological role as filter feeders, actively pumping seawater through their bodies to extract plankton and nutrients. This process helps maintain water clarity and quality in their habitat.

Food Source: They are an important food source for various coastal predators, including birds, fish, and crabs. Their abundance makes them a key link in the coastal food web.

Stabilization of Sediments: By burrowing into the sand, coquinas contribute to sediment stabilization and can influence the dynamics of beach erosion and accretion.

Cultural and Historical Importance
Coquinas have a rich history intertwined with human cultures, especially among indigenous coastal communities. In some traditions, coquina shells were used as decorative elements in jewelry or as currency. Their presence in archaeological sites along the Georgia coast underscores their enduring significance to past civilizations.

Conservation and Management

While coquinas are currently not considered threatened, their populations can be sensitive to changes in coastal habitats, including pollution and habitat destruction. Conservation efforts often focus on preserving the integrity of coastal ecosystems through sustainable management practices and monitoring of water quality.

In conclusion, coquinas, represented by Donax variabilis, are not merely shells but integral components of Georgia's coastal ecosystems. Their vibrant colors, ecological roles, and historical significance make them a fascinating subject of study and admiration. By understanding and appreciating these small but mighty bivalves, we deepen our appreciation for the intricate balance of life along the shores of Georgia and beyond.

Scotch Bonnet (Phalium granulatum)

The Scotch Bonnet, scientifically known as Phalium granulatum, is a fascinating marine mollusk that holds significant interest among collectors and beachcombers alike in the coastal regions of Georgia. Renowned for its distinctive shape and striking coloration, this seashell species has captured the attention of naturalists and enthusiasts for generations.

Physical Characteristics

The Scotch Bonnet shell typically measures between 1 to 4 inches in length, featuring a conical shape with a pronounced spire and a smooth, glossy surface. Its coloration ranges from pale cream to vibrant orange, often adorned with intricate patterns of darker spots or bands. The shell's outer lip is thick and flared, while the interior reveals a smooth and iridescent nacre, adding to its allure.

Habitat and Distribution

In Georgia, Scotch Bonnets are commonly found along the sandy shores and shallow waters of barrier islands and coastal beaches. They prefer warm, tropical waters and are frequently encountered after storms or during low tides when shells are washed ashore. Their distribution extends throughout the southeastern United States, from North Carolina to Florida, encompassing a range of marine environments conducive to their growth.

Ecological Significance

As part of the marine ecosystem, Scotch Bonnets play a crucial role in nutrient cycling and sediment dynamics. Their presence on beaches contributes to the overall biodiversity of coastal habitats, supporting various organisms that rely on shells for shelter and protection. Additionally, their vibrant colors and patterns make them a subject of study in evolutionary biology and shell morphology.

Cultural and Recreational Importance

Beyond their ecological role, Scotch Bonnets hold cultural significance as prized collectibles and decorative items. Beachgoers often search for these shells along the tideline, appreciating their aesthetic appeal and unique characteristics. In Georgia, the discovery of a well-preserved Scotch Bonnet shell is a cherished moment for shell collectors and enthusiasts who value the natural beauty of coastal ecosystems.

Conservation and Management

While Scotch Bonnets are not considered threatened or endangered, conservation efforts are crucial to preserving their habitats and ensuring sustainable shell collection practices. Coastal development, pollution, and climate change pose potential threats to their populations, underscoring the importance of responsible environmental stewardship and marine conservation initiatives.

In conclusion, the Scotch Bonnet (Phalium granulatum) stands as a prominent symbol of Georgia's coastal biodiversity, admired for its distinctive appearance and ecological significance. Whether encountered during a leisurely beach stroll or studied in scientific research, this seashell species continues to captivate and inspire appreciation for the natural wonders found along the shores of the southeastern United States. Its presence reminds us of the interconnectedness between land and sea, urging us to preserve and protect these valuable ecosystems for future generations to enjoy.

Rare and Endangered Seashells of Georgia
Georgia Pigtoe (Pleurobema hanleyianum)

The Georgia Pigtoe, scientifically known as Pleurobema hanleyianum, is a freshwater mussel species endemic to Georgia, USA. It belongs to the family Unionidae, which comprises freshwater mussels commonly found in rivers and streams across North America. However, the Georgia Pigtoe is distinguished by its limited range and endangered status, making it a focal point for conservation efforts.

Physical Characteristics

The Georgia Pigtoe displays a distinctive shell morphology. Typically, its shell is elongated and oval–shaped, with a smooth surface and a glossy appearance. The coloration varies, often ranging from light brown to yellowish–green, sometimes with darker concentric rings or patches. The hinge line of the shell is straight, and the posterior end is bluntly rounded.

Habitat and Distribution

This rare mussel species is primarily found in a few select rivers and streams within the state of Georgia. It prefers habitats with clean, flowing water and stable substrates such as sand or gravel. The Georgia Pigtoe is known to inhabit the Flint River basin and its tributaries, as well as a few other river systems within Georgia. However, due to habitat degradation and other environmental pressures, its range has significantly declined over the years.

Conservation Status

The conservation status of Pleurobema hanleyianum is critically endangered. The main threats to its survival include habitat loss and degradation due to damming, pollution, sedimentation, and changes in water quality and flow patterns. Additionally, like many freshwater mussels, the Georgia Pigtoe is sensitive to changes in its environment, including temperature fluctuations and invasive species.

Efforts to conserve the Georgia Pigtoe involve various strategies, such as habitat restoration, water quality improvement, and captive breeding programs. Conservation organizations work closely with state and federal agencies to monitor populations, conduct research on their biology and ecology, and implement protective measures.

Importance in the Ecosystem

Freshwater mussels play a vital role in maintaining ecosystem health. They filter water to feed, which helps to improve water quality by removing organic particles and contaminants. Additionally, mussels serve as indicators of water quality; their presence or absence can signify the overall health of aquatic ecosystems.

The decline of the Georgia Pigtoe and other freshwater mussel species can have far-reaching ecological consequences. Their disappearance could disrupt food webs and impact other aquatic organisms that rely on them for habitat and food sources.

Conservation Efforts and Challenges

Conserving the Georgia Pigtoe presents several challenges. The fragmented distribution of remaining populations makes it difficult to protect all habitats effectively. Moreover, addressing the root causes of habitat degradation requires collaborative efforts across different sectors, including government agencies, conservation groups, landowners, and the general public.

Public awareness and education also play crucial roles in conservation efforts. By raising awareness about the plight of the Georgia Pigtoe and other freshwater mussels, stakeholders can advocate for policy changes, support habitat restoration projects, and promote responsible environmental practices.

The Georgia Pigtoe, Pleurobema hanleyianum, represents not only a unique species of freshwater mussel but also a symbol of the challenges faced by aquatic biodiversity in Georgia. Its rarity and endangered status underscore the urgent need for conservation action to preserve not just this species, but the health and integrity of freshwater ecosystems as a whole. Through collaborative efforts and sustained commitment to conservation, there remains hope for the recovery and long–term survival of the Georgia Pigtoe and other endangered seashells of Georgia.

Spectacled Bear Paw (Cyclonaias tuberculata)

The Spectacled Bear Paw, scientifically known as Cyclonaias tuberculata, is a remarkable and endangered species of freshwater mussel found in the waterways of Georgia, particularly notable for its distinct appearance and ecological significance. This comprehensive overview delves into its taxonomy, habitat, conservation status, and importance within Georgia's ecosystem.

Taxonomy and Appearance

Cyclonaias tuberculata belongs to the Unionidae family, commonly known as freshwater mussels. Its shell is characterized by a robust, oval shape with prominent ridges and concentric growth lines, resembling the pattern found on a bear paw hence its name. The shell typically ranges in color from light brown to dark green, often displaying a lustrous sheen when freshly extracted from riverbeds.

Habitat and Distribution

Historically, the Spectacled Bear Paw thrived in the larger river systems and tributaries of Georgia, preferring clean, fast-flowing waters with sandy or gravelly substrates. However, due to habitat degradation, pollution, and changes in water quality, its population has sharply declined. Today, it is primarily found in isolated pockets within certain river basins, such as the Altamaha and Savannah Rivers, where conservation efforts are focused.

Ecological Importance

As filter feeders, freshwater mussels like Cyclonaias tuberculata play a crucial role in maintaining water quality by filtering and purifying large volumes of water. Their presence helps to control algae levels and sediment, contributing to the overall health of aquatic ecosystems. Furthermore, their shells provide habitat and substrate for various aquatic organisms, enhancing biodiversity within Georgia's waterways.

Conservation Status and Threats

The Spectacled Bear Paw is listed as endangered under state and federal legislation due to ongoing threats to its habitat and population. Major threats include habitat destruction from damming, sedimentation, pollution from agricultural runoff and industrial activities, and the introduction of invasive species. Conservation efforts involve habitat restoration, water quality management, and public awareness campaigns to mitigate these threats and promote the recovery of mussel populations.

Conservation Efforts

Numerous organizations, including state wildlife agencies, conservation groups, and academic institutions, are actively involved in the conservation of Cyclonaias tuberculata. Efforts focus on monitoring population trends, restoring degraded habitats, conducting research on mussel biology and ecology, and engaging in outreach and education to raise awareness about the importance of freshwater mussel conservation.

The Spectacled Bear Paw, Cyclonaias tuberculata, stands as a poignant symbol of the challenges facing freshwater ecosystems in Georgia. Its rarity and ecological significance underscore the urgent need for concerted conservation efforts to ensure the survival of this species and the health of its habitat. By addressing the threats facing freshwater mussels and their habitats, we can strive towards a future where these vital organisms thrive once again in Georgia's waterways.

In summary, the Spectacled Bear Paw serves not only as a unique and visually striking seashell but also as a critical indicator of the health of Georgia's freshwater ecosystems, highlighting the interconnectedness of biodiversity and environmental conservation efforts.

Pale Lilliput (Toxolasma lividum)
The Pale Lilliput, scientifically known as Toxolasma lividum, stands as a testament to the delicate balance of aquatic ecosystems and the challenges faced by endangered species. Found primarily in the waters surrounding Georgia, this freshwater mussel species plays a crucial role in maintaining water quality and supporting biodiversity. However, due to various human-induced pressures, the Pale Lilliput has

become increasingly rare, highlighting the importance of conservation efforts.

Physical Characteristics

The Pale Lilliput is a small freshwater mussel, typically reaching lengths between 1.5 to 2.5 centimeters. Its shell is thin and fragile, with a pale yellow to light brown coloration, often adorned with subtle, irregular growth lines. The shape of the shell is elongated and slightly triangular, tapering towards both ends. These features make it distinct from other mussel species found in the region.

Habitat and Distribution

Toxolasma lividum inhabits freshwater rivers, streams, and creeks with sandy or gravelly bottoms, where it burrows into the substrate to filter feed on microscopic organisms and organic debris. Historically, the Pale Lilliput was more widespread across the southeastern United States, including Georgia. However, habitat destruction, pollution, and changes in water quality have significantly reduced its range and population size.

Conservation Status

The Pale Lilliput is categorized as endangered by both state and federal conservation agencies. This designation reflects the critical need for immediate action to protect and restore its habitats. Efforts to conserve this species include habitat restoration projects, water quality improvement initiatives, and captive breeding programs aimed at boosting wild populations.

Threats

Several factors contribute to the decline of the Pale Lilliput population:

Habitat Destruction: Urbanization, agriculture, and damming alter water flow and quality, destroying critical mussel habitats.

Pollution: Runoff containing sediment, chemicals, and nutrients negatively impacts water quality, affecting the health of mussels.

Invasive Species: Non-native species outcompete native mussels for resources and can parasitize them, further reducing populations.

Climate Change: Altered precipitation patterns and rising temperatures can disrupt mussel reproduction and survival.

Conservation Efforts

Conservation efforts for the Pale Lilliput focus on:

Habitat Restoration: Reintroducing native vegetation, restoring natural river processes, and removing barriers to water flow.

Water Quality Improvement: Monitoring and reducing pollutants entering waterways through regulations and community initiatives.

Public Awareness: Educating communities about the importance of freshwater mussels and encouraging sustainable practices.

Legislation and Regulation: Enforcing laws protecting freshwater habitats and species, including the Pale Lilliput.

Importance to Ecosystem

As a filter feeder, the Pale Lilliput plays a crucial role in maintaining water quality. By removing particles and nutrients from the water, it helps clarify aquatic habitats, benefiting other organisms such as fish and aquatic insects. Its decline could disrupt the balance of these ecosystems, leading to cascading effects on biodiversity and water resources.

The Pale Lilliput, Toxolasma lividum, serves as a poignant example of the challenges faced by endangered species in Georgia's freshwater ecosystems. While conservation efforts are underway, the species remains at risk due to ongoing threats. Protecting the Pale Lilliput requires collaborative action among scientists, policymakers, and local communities to ensure the health of its habitat and the preservation of its important ecological role for future generations. Efforts to conserve the Pale Lilliput contribute not only to its survival but also to the broader health and resilience of Georgia's aquatic environments.

Conservation Efforts and Challenges

Seashells, often admired for their intricate beauty and ecological significance, play a crucial role in Georgia's coastal ecosystem. The conservation efforts surrounding these delicate treasures are essential to maintain biodiversity and ecosystem balance. However, they face numerous challenges that threaten their existence and the broader marine environment.

Ecological Importance of Seashells

Seashells are more than just decorative objects; they serve several ecological functions:

Habitat and Shelter: Many marine organisms, such as hermit crabs and small fish, use seashells as shelter and protection from predators.

Nutrient Cycling: Calcium carbonate, the primary component of seashells, plays a role in buffering ocean acidity and cycling essential nutrients.

Indicator Species: The presence and condition of certain seashell species can indicate the health of coastal ecosystems, making them valuable indicators for environmental monitoring.

Conservation Efforts

Conservation efforts in Georgia focus on preserving seashells and their habitats through various strategies:

Marine Protected Areas (MPAs): Designated areas where seashells are protected from overharvesting and habitat degradation.

Education and Awareness: Programs aimed at educating the public about the ecological importance of seashells and the need for conservation.

Scientific Research: Studying seashell populations, their habitats, and the impacts of human activities to inform conservation strategies.

Legislation and Regulation: Laws and regulations that limit the collection of certain seashell species or restrict activities that harm their habitats.

Habitat Restoration: Initiatives to restore seagrass beds, oyster reefs, and other habitats that support seashell populations.

Challenges Facing Seashells in Georgia

Despite conservation efforts, seashells in Georgia face several challenges:

Habitat Loss and Degradation: Coastal development, pollution, and climate change contribute to habitat loss and degradation, reducing suitable habitats for seashells.

Overharvesting: The collection of seashells for commercial trade, souvenirs, or crafts can deplete local populations, especially for species with attractive shells.

Climate Change: Rising sea temperatures, ocean acidification, and changes in currents affect seashell growth, reproduction, and overall health.

Invasive Species: The introduction of non-native species can outcompete native seashell species or disrupt their habitats.

Pollution: Chemical pollutants and marine debris (such as plastics) can directly harm seashells or their habitats.

Future Directions

To enhance seashell conservation in Georgia, future efforts should focus on:

Integrated Management Approaches: Collaborative efforts among government agencies, scientists, conservation organizations, and local communities to implement comprehensive conservation strategies.

Adaptation to Climate Change: Developing strategies to mitigate and adapt to the impacts of climate change on seashell populations and their habitats.

Community Engagement: Involving local communities in conservation efforts through citizen science, sustainable tourism practices, and community-based conservation initiatives.

Monitoring and Research: Continued research to monitor seashell populations, assess the effectiveness of conservation measures, and understand emerging threats.

Policy Development: Strengthening policies and regulations to ensure sustainable use of seashell resources and protect critical habitats.

In conclusion, while seashells in Georgia face significant challenges, concerted conservation efforts can help preserve these valuable marine resources for future generations. By addressing these challenges through scientific research, education, community engagement, and effective policy, we can ensure that seashells continue to thrive and contribute to the health of coastal ecosystems in Georgia and beyond.

Map 1: Coastal regions of Georgia

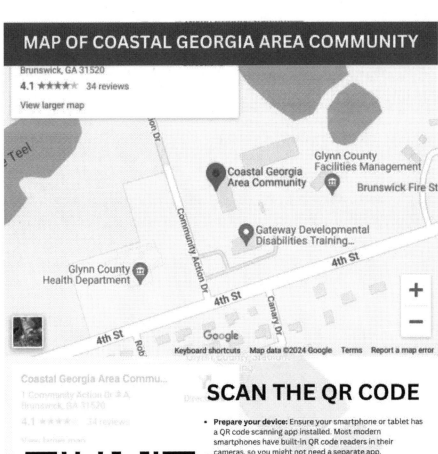

SCAN THE QR CODE

- **Prepare your device:** Ensure your smartphone or tablet has a QR code scanning app installed. Most modern smartphones have built-in QR code readers in their cameras, so you might not need a separate app.

- **Open the QR code scanner:** Launch the QR code scanning app or open your smartphone's camera.

- **Position the QR code:** Hold your device steady and position the QR code within the viewfinder or camera frame. Make sure the QR code is well-lit and not obscured.

- **Scan the QR code:** If you're using a dedicated app, align the QR code within the app's scanning area and it should automatically scan. If you're using your smartphone camera, simply point it at the QR code. Most smartphones will recognize the QR code automatically and provide a notification or a link.

- **Interpret the result:** Once scanned, your device will typically interpret the QR code's data. This could be a URL, text, contact information, or other types of data embedded in the QR code. Follow the prompts on your device to proceed with the information provided.

MAP OF COASTAL REGIONAL COMMISSION

31305

1.5 ★★★★★ 11 reviews

View larger map

Coastal Regional Commission

Coastal Regional Commission of...

Coastal Dr SW

God's Oceans

Google
Keyboard shortcuts   Map data ©2024   Terms   Report a map error

SCAN THE QR CODE

- **Prepare your device:** Ensure your smartphone or tablet has a QR code scanning app installed. Most modern smartphones have built-in QR code readers in their cameras, so you might not need a separate app.

- **Open the QR code scanner:** Launch the QR code scanning app or open your smartphone's camera.

- **Position the QR code:** Hold your device steady and position the QR code within the viewfinder or camera frame. Make sure the QR code is well-lit and not obscured.

- **Scan the QR code:** If you're using a dedicated app, align the QR code within the app's scanning area and it should automatically scan. If you're using your smartphone camera, simply point it at the QR code. Most smartphones will recognize the QR code automatically and provide a notification or a link.

- **Interpret the result:** Once scanned, your device will typically interpret the QR code's data. This could be a URL, text, contact information, or other types of data embedded in the QR code. Follow the prompts on your device to proceed with the information provided.

109

CHAPTER THREE

Seashells of the Carolinas

Coastal Habitats of the Carolinas

The coastal habitats of the Carolinas are a captivating blend of diverse ecosystems that foster a myriad of seashell species. Stretching from the barrier islands to the estuarine marshes, these environments provide unique niches for mollusks and other marine organisms, shaping the rich tapestry of seashells found along these shores.

Barrier Islands: Dynamic Shores of Diversity

The barrier islands off the coasts of North and South Carolina serve as the first line of defense against oceanic forces while nurturing a wealth of seashell diversity. These islands, formed by the relentless forces of wind and waves, create a mosaic of habitats including sandy beaches, dunes, and salt marshes.

Sandy Beaches: The wide, sandy beaches of the barrier islands are prime hunting grounds for beachcombers seeking treasures like whelks, conchs, and sand dollars. The constant reshaping of the shoreline by tides and storms ensures a continuous turnover of shells, each telling a story of its journey from deep waters to the shore.

Dunes: Beyond the beaches, dunes provide a unique habitat for specialized species such as the delicate wentletrap or the intricately patterned auger shell. These shells often exhibit adaptations that help them survive in the shifting sands and harsh coastal winds.

Salt Marshes: Edging the barrier islands are expansive salt marshes, where brackish waters create a haven for mollusks like marsh periwinkles and ribbed mussels. The shells found here, often smaller and more robust, reflect the adaptations necessary to thrive in fluctuating salinity and tidal conditions.

Estuarine Environments: Nurseries of the Sea

Moving inland, the estuarine environments of the Carolinas play a crucial role in the lifecycle of many seashell species. Estuaries, where freshwater rivers meet the salty ocean, form complex ecosystems characterized by tidal mudflats, oyster reefs, and submerged aquatic vegetation.

Mudflats: Extending from the intertidal zone into shallow waters, mudflats host shells such as razor clams and coquina clams. These bivalves and gastropods bury themselves in the nutrient-rich mud, feeding on organic matter brought in by tidal currents.

Oyster Reefs: Oyster reefs not only provide a critical habitat for oysters but also create a substrate for barnacles, periwinkles, and other shell-bearing organisms. The intricate textures of these shells reflect their adaptation to the harsh conditions of the reef environment.

Seagrass Meadows: Within the estuarine waters, seagrass meadows form verdant underwater landscapes that support a diverse array of seashell species. From the elaborate spirals of moon snails to the iridescent hues of jingle shells, these shells are often prized for their beauty and ecological significance.

Conservation and Appreciation

The coastal habitats of the Carolinas face numerous challenges, including coastal development, pollution, and climate change. Conservation efforts are crucial to preserving these unique ecosystems and ensuring the future abundance of seashells. Organizations and researchers work diligently to monitor populations, restore habitats, and educate the public about the importance of coastal conservation.

Understanding the intricate relationships between seashells and their habitats enhances our appreciation for these coastal treasures. Whether collecting shells along the shorelines or studying them in their natural habitats, each encounter with a seashell tells a story of resilience and adaptation in the dynamic coastal ecosystems of the Carolinas.

In conclusion, the coastal habitats of the Carolinas offer a rich tapestry of environments that support a diverse array of seashells. From the sandy shores of barrier islands to the intricate ecosystems of estuarine waters, each habitat plays a vital role in shaping the seashell diversity found along these shores. As stewards of these coastal environments, we have a responsibility to conserve and protect these habitats for future generations to continue enjoying and studying the seashells of the Carolinas.

Common Seashell Species in the Carolinas
Scotch Bonnet (Phalium granulatum)
The Scotch Bonnet (Phalium granulatum) stands as an iconic symbol of the diverse marine life found along the Carolinas' coastal regions. Its distinctive

appearance and rich history within the realm of seashell collectors and enthusiasts make it a prized find among beachcombers. This comprehensive guide explores the Scotch Bonnet's characteristics, habitat, significance, and allure among those who appreciate the natural beauty of seashells.

Physical Description:

The Scotch Bonnet shell is characterized by its unique shape and vibrant colors. It typically features a tall, conical spire with a smooth surface adorned by intricate spiral ridges. Its aperture, or opening, is wide and flares outwards, often displaying a striking blend of hues ranging from creamy whites to shades of orange, pink, and sometimes deep red. These colors can vary based on environmental factors and the specific subspecies found in different areas.

Habitat and Distribution:

Phalium granulatum, commonly known as the Scotch Bonnet, inhabits the warm coastal waters along the southeastern United States, including the Carolinas. These shells are often found in shallow waters near sandy or muddy bottoms, where they feed on small marine organisms and algae. Their distribution is influenced by water temperature and nutrient availability, making certain coastal areas particularly favorable for their growth.

Ecological Role:

As part of the marine ecosystem, Scotch Bonnets play a role in nutrient cycling and biodiversity. Their presence indicates a healthy marine environment and contributes to the food web by serving as both predator and prey to various marine organisms. Conservation efforts often focus on protecting habitats where these shells thrive, ensuring the sustainability of their populations for future generations.

Cultural and Collectible Significance:

Beyond their ecological importance, Scotch Bonnets hold cultural significance as prized collectibles and symbols of coastal beauty. Collectors and enthusiasts are drawn to their aesthetic appeal and rarity, with certain color variations and patterns being highly sought after. In the Carolinas, local artisans may incorporate Scotch Bonnets into crafts or jewelry, further highlighting their cultural value and connection to the region's maritime heritage.

Conservation and Protection:

Due to their popularity among collectors and the potential impact of habitat degradation, Scotch Bonnets face conservation challenges. Efforts to protect their habitats and regulate shell collecting help ensure that these beautiful creatures continue to thrive in their natural environment. Awareness campaigns educate beachgoers about responsible shell-collecting practices, promoting sustainable interactions with marine ecosystems.

In conclusion, the Scotch Bonnet (Phalium granulatum) stands as a captivating example of the natural beauty and ecological diversity found in the Carolinas' coastal waters. Its distinctive appearance, cultural significance, and ecological role underscore the importance of preserving marine habitats and appreciating the wonders of the natural world. Whether admired for its striking colors or studied for its ecological contributions, the Scotch Bonnet continues to enchant and inspire those who encounter it along the sandy shores of the Carolinas.

Wentletrap (Epitonium scalare)

The Wentletrap, scientifically known as Epitonium scalare, is a marvel of marine mollusks found along the coastal shores of the Carolinas. Renowned for its intricate spiral structure and delicate appearance, this seashell belongs to the family Epitoniidae, which includes a diverse array of species characterized by their elongated shells and fine sculptural details.

Physical Characteristics

The Epitonium scalare typically measures between 1 to 2 inches in length, though larger specimens up to 3 inches have been recorded. Its shell is slender, elongated, and gracefully spiraled, resembling a miniature turret or a spiral staircase. The shell's surface is adorned with fine, raised ridges and spiral grooves, giving it a ribbed appearance that enhances its elegance.

The coloration of the Wentletrap shell varies, ranging from creamy white to pale beige or light brown. Some specimens may exhibit subtle banding or color gradations, adding to their visual allure. Despite its delicate appearance, the shell of Epitonium scalare is surprisingly durable, reflecting the evolutionary adaptations that enable it to withstand the pressures of its marine environment.

Natural Habitat and Distribution

Epitonium scalare is commonly found in shallow coastal waters along the Atlantic coast of the United States, including the Carolinas. These seashells inhabit sandy or muddy substrates, often near coral reefs or rocky outcrops where they can feed on microscopic organisms and detritus. Their distribution extends from North Carolina southward to Florida, thriving in temperate to subtropical waters characterized by moderate wave action and sufficient food sources.

Ecological Role

In its natural habitat, the Wentletrap plays a vital ecological role as part of the marine food web. As a filter feeder, it helps maintain water clarity by consuming planktonic organisms and organic particles suspended in the water column. Additionally, the shells of deceased Wentletraps contribute to the calcium carbonate cycle, eventually breaking down and becoming part of the sedimentary layers of the ocean floor.

Cultural and Artistic Significance

Beyond its ecological importance, Epitonium scalare holds cultural and artistic significance. Throughout history, Wentletrap shells have been prized by collectors and artisans for their exquisite beauty and intricate form. They have inspired artists and craftspeople to create jewelry, decorative objects, and even architectural motifs that celebrate the elegance of nature's designs.

Conservation and Management

While not currently under significant threat, the conservation of Epitonium scalare and its habitat is important for maintaining the biodiversity of coastal ecosystems. Conservation efforts focus on preserving coastal habitats, minimizing pollution, and promoting sustainable fishing practices that do not harm marine mollusks or their habitats.

In summary, the Wentletrap (Epitonium scalare) stands as a testament to the natural beauty and intricate design found within the marine environment of the Carolinas. Its delicate spiral shell, ecological role, and cultural significance make it a beloved symbol of coastal biodiversity and natural wonder. By understanding and appreciating the Wentletrap, we can foster a deeper appreciation for the intricate ecosystems that support marine life along the Atlantic seaboard.

Whether admired for its aesthetic appeal, studied for its ecological contributions, or cherished as a collector's item, the Wentletrap continues to captivate the imaginations of those who encounter its timeless beauty along the shores of the Carolinas.

Nutmeg (Cancellaria reticulata)
Nutmeg, scientifically known as Cancellaria reticulata, is a charming and widely recognized seashell species found along the shores of the Carolinas. Its distinctive

appearance and prevalence make it a favorite among beachcombers and shell enthusiasts alike. This article explores the characteristics, habitat, ecological significance, and cultural relevance of the Nutmeg seashell in the coastal regions of the Carolinas.

Characteristics

The Nutmeg seashell is characterized by its small to medium size, typically ranging from 1 to 2 inches in length. Its shape is elongated and spindle–like, with a smooth, glossy surface adorned by intricate patterns of fine ridges and delicate, net–like markings. These features give the shell a distinct and elegant appearance, often compared to the rich brown color of the nutmeg spice, hence its common name.

Habitat

Cancellaria reticulata thrives in the shallow coastal waters of the Carolinas, particularly along sandy or muddy substrates where it can bury itself partially. These shells are often found washed ashore after storms or during low tide, making them accessible to beachcombers. Nutmegs are known for their preference for warmer waters and can be found from the Outer Banks of North Carolina to the coastal areas of South Carolina.

Ecological Role

In its natural habitat, the Nutmeg seashell plays a significant ecological role. As a part of the marine ecosystem, it contributes to nutrient cycling and provides habitats for small organisms such as tiny crabs and algae. The shells themselves also serve as homes for hermit crabs, offering protection and camouflage from predators.

Cultural Significance

Beyond its ecological importance, the Nutmeg seashell holds cultural significance in the Carolinas. It is often collected by beachgoers and shell collectors who appreciate its aesthetic beauty and unique patterns. In coastal communities, shells like the Nutmeg are sometimes used in crafts and local artwork, reflecting the region's deep connection to the sea and its natural resources.

Conservation

While Nutmeg seashells are currently abundant in the Carolinas, they, like many other marine species, face threats from habitat destruction, pollution, and climate change. Responsible shell-collecting practices and efforts to preserve coastal habitats are crucial to ensuring the continued health of populations like Cancellaria reticulata.

The Nutmeg seashell, with its striking appearance and ecological importance, exemplifies the rich biodiversity found along the shores of the Carolinas. As beachcombers and conservationists alike marvel at its beauty and significance, efforts to protect coastal environments become all the more imperative. By understanding and appreciating species like the Nutmeg, we deepen our connection to the natural world and inspire conservation actions that benefit both marine life and future generations of shell enthusiasts.

Turkey Wing (Arca zebra)

The Turkey Wing (Arca zebra) is a striking and widely recognized seashell species found along the coasts of the Carolinas, adding a distinct charm to the region's beaches. Known for its unique appearance and ecological significance, this bivalve mollusk holds a special place in marine ecosystems and human fascination alike.

Physical Characteristics:

The Turkey Wing shell is characterized by its smooth, elongated shape resembling the outline of a bird's wing, hence its common name. The shells typically range in size from 2 to 4 inches in length, with a glossy exterior that showcases a combination of pale yellows, pinks, and oranges, often with intricate patterns of zigzags or chevrons. The inner surface of the shell is smooth and pearlescent, adding to its allure when found washed ashore.

Habitat and Distribution:

Arca zebra inhabits shallow coastal waters and can be found buried in sandy or muddy substrates, often in intertidal zones where it can filter–feed on plankton and organic matter suspended in the water. Along the Carolinas' coastline, these shells are frequently discovered during low tide, particularly in areas with moderate wave action that helps to dislodge them from the substrate.

Ecological Role:

As filter feeders, Turkey Wing clams play a vital role in maintaining water quality by filtering out algae and other particulate matter from the water column. They contribute to the overall health of coastal ecosystems by influencing nutrient cycling and supporting the diversity of marine life in their habitats.

Cultural Significance:

Beyond their ecological role, Turkey Wing shells have historical and cultural significance. Indigenous peoples of the region, such as the Native American tribes of the Carolinas, used these shells for decorative purposes and as tools in various cultural practices. Today, they continue to be prized by collectors and beachcombers alike for their aesthetic appeal and unique patterns.

Conservation Status:

While Turkey Wing shells are not currently considered endangered, their populations can be vulnerable to habitat destruction and pollution. Conservation efforts focused on preserving coastal habitats and monitoring water quality are crucial to ensuring their continued presence along the Carolinas' shores.

Human Interaction:

The shells of Arca zebra are frequently collected by beachgoers, shell enthusiasts, and artisans who use them in crafts and jewelry. Collectors need to adhere to local regulations and ethical guidelines to minimize the impact on natural populations and ecosystems.

The Turkey Wing (Arca zebra) stands out among the common seashell species of the Carolinas for its distinctive appearance, ecological importance, and cultural relevance. Whether admired for its beauty, studied for its role in marine ecosystems, or used in creative endeavors, this shell exemplifies the intricate relationship between nature and human culture along the Atlantic coast. As guardians of our coastal environments, we play a pivotal role in ensuring that future generations can continue to enjoy and appreciate the natural treasures found in our seas.

Angel Wing (Cyrtopleura costata)

The Angel Wing, scientifically known as Cyrtopleura costata, is a distinctive and striking seashell found along the shores of the Carolinas. Its name derives from its delicate, wing–like shape and pearly–white coloration, resembling the graceful wings of an angel. This species holds a significant place in the local marine ecosystem and has captivated beachcombers and naturalists alike with its beauty and ecological importance.

Physical Characteristics

Shell Shape and Size:

The Angel Wing shell is elongated and narrow, typically growing up to 6 inches in length, although larger specimens have been recorded.

Its shape resembles a flattened, elongated rectangle, tapering towards both ends, giving it a sleek and aerodynamic appearance.

Coloration and Surface:

The shell is predominantly smooth with fine, concentric ridges that radiate from the hinge area towards the outer edges.

When freshly washed ashore, the Angel Wing exhibits a glossy, iridescent white exterior, often adorned with subtle hints of pink or lavender.

Internal Structure:

Internally, the shell reveals a mother-of-pearl sheen, displaying shades of silver, pink, and blue in an intricate pattern.

The hinge area is distinctive, featuring teeth-like structures that facilitate the clam's attachment to submerged surfaces.

Habitat and Distribution

Natural Habitat:

Angel Wings are primarily found in shallow coastal waters, buried just beneath the sandy or muddy substrate.

They prefer areas with moderate currents where they can filter-feed on plankton and detritus carried by the water.

Geographical Distribution:

Along the Atlantic coast of the United States, the Angel Wing is commonly encountered from North Carolina down through South Carolina.

They are also found in parts of the Gulf of Mexico, extending to the Yucatan Peninsula in Mexico.

Ecological Significance

Filter-Feeding Role:

As filter feeders, Angel Wings play a crucial ecological role in maintaining water clarity and quality by filtering small particles and organic matter from the water column.

Habitat for Other Species:

The presence of Angel Wings provides habitat and shelter for small marine organisms such as small fish, crustaceans, and juvenile mollusks.

Indicator Species:

Their presence or absence can serve as indicators of environmental health, reflecting changes in water quality and ecosystem dynamics.

Cultural and Recreational Importance

Beachcombing and Collecting:

Angel Wings are highly sought after by beachcombers and collectors for their elegant appearance and relative rarity.

Local artisans often use Angel Wing shells in crafting jewelry and decorative items, adding cultural value to these shells.

Scientific Research:

Scientists study Angel Wings to understand their growth patterns, reproductive biology, and ecological interactions, contributing to broader marine conservation efforts.

Conservation Status and Threats

Conservation Concerns:

Habitat destruction due to coastal development and pollution poses a significant threat to Angel Wing populations.

Climate change–induced ocean acidification and warming may also impact their distribution and survival.

Conservation Efforts:

Efforts to protect coastal habitats and implement sustainable management practices are crucial for safeguarding Angel Wings and their associated ecosystems.

The Angel Wing (Cyrtopleura costata) stands out not only for its striking appearance but also for its ecological importance and cultural significance along the Carolinas' coastlines. As stewards of marine biodiversity, it is imperative to recognize and protect these emblematic seashells to ensure they continue to inspire wonder and contribute to the health of coastal ecosystems for future generations.

Unique Seashell Finds in the Carolinas
Carolina Fan (Gari tellinella)

The Carolina Fan, scientifically known as Gari tellinella, is a fascinating species of seashell found along the coastlines of the Carolinas, particularly notable for its distinctive appearance and ecological significance. This small bivalve mollusk belongs to the family Psammobiidae and is cherished by beachcombers and collectors alike for its intricate patterns and delicate structure.

Physical Characteristics

The Carolina Fan shell is typically small, measuring around 1 to 2 centimeters in length. Its shape is elongated and narrow, resembling a flattened triangle or trapezoid when viewed from the side. The shell's exterior features prominent ridges or ribs that run parallel to its length, creating a fan-like pattern that gives the species its common name, "Carolina Fan."

The coloration of Gari tellinella shells varies widely, ranging from pale cream or white to shades of yellow, orange, or brown. Some specimens may exhibit subtle banding or streaks along the ribs, adding to their aesthetic appeal.

Habitat and Distribution

Carolina Fans are primarily found in shallow coastal waters along the Atlantic Ocean, from North Carolina to South Carolina. They inhabit sandy or muddy substrates, often buried just beneath the surface where they feed on microscopic plankton and detritus. These bivalves are filter feeders, using their specialized gills to extract nutrients from the surrounding water.

During low tide, Carolina Fans may be exposed on the beach, making them accessible to beachcombers and enthusiasts interested in collecting seashells. Their presence in these intertidal zones contributes to the rich biodiversity of the region's coastal ecosystems.

Ecological Importance

As part of the diverse marine life of the Carolinas, Gari tellinella plays a significant role in the local ecosystem. They are preyed upon by various shorebirds, fish, and crustaceans, contributing to the food web dynamics of coastal habitats. Their filter–feeding behavior also helps maintain water quality by removing particulate matter and excess nutrients from the water column.

Conservation efforts often focus on preserving the habitats where Carolina Fans thrive, including estuaries, mudflats, and sandy shores. These efforts are crucial for maintaining the overall health and biodiversity of the region's marine environments.

Cultural and Recreational Significance

Beyond their ecological importance, Carolina Fans hold cultural and recreational significance for residents and visitors of the Carolinas. They are frequently collected for their aesthetic value, with enthusiasts admiring the shells' unique patterns and colors. Many beachgoers enjoy searching for these and other seashell species as a relaxing pastime, contributing to the region's tourism and coastal economy.

Conservation and Management

Due to factors such as habitat loss, pollution, and climate change, the conservation of Carolina Fan populations is increasingly important. Conservation efforts include habitat restoration projects, monitoring of water quality, and public education on responsible shell-collecting practices. By raising awareness about the ecological roles of these bivalves, conservationists aim to ensure their continued presence in the coastal ecosystems of the Carolinas for future generations to enjoy.

The Carolina Fan (Gari tellinella) exemplifies the beauty and ecological significance of seashell species found in the Carolinas. Its distinctive appearance, habitat preferences, and role in coastal ecosystems make it a valuable species both scientifically and culturally. By understanding and appreciating the Carolina Fan, we can contribute to the conservation of coastal biodiversity and promote sustainable practices that benefit marine environments as a whole.

Emerald Gem Clam (Gemophos tinctures)

The Emerald Gem Clam, scientifically known as Gemophos tinctus, is a mesmerizing marine mollusk found along the pristine shores of the Carolinas. Renowned for its exquisite beauty and rarity, this species captivates beachcombers and marine enthusiasts alike with its distinct emerald–green hues and delicate shell structure.

Physical Characteristics

The Emerald Gem Clam is relatively small, typically measuring between 1 to 2 inches in length. Its shell, the most striking feature, boasts a glossy surface adorned with vibrant green patterns that shimmer under sunlight, reminiscent of the precious gemstone after which it is named. The shell's shape is elongated and slender, tapering gently towards the hinge, where it forms a smooth and symmetrical closure.

Habitat and Distribution

These enchanting clams are predominantly found in shallow coastal waters along the southeastern United States, particularly in the Carolinas. They inhabit sandy or muddy substrates near the intertidal zone, where they burrow to seek shelter and feed on microscopic organisms and organic matter present in the sediment.

Ecological Significance

As filter feeders, Emerald Gem Clams play a crucial role in maintaining water quality and ecosystem balance. By filtering water to extract nutrients, they contribute to the overall health of coastal habitats, thereby supporting the diverse array of marine life that depends on clean, nutrient–rich environments.

Rarity and Conservation

The Emerald Gem Clam is considered a rare find among seashell enthusiasts due to its limited distribution and specific habitat requirements. Conservation efforts are crucial to preserving populations of these delicate creatures, as coastal development and pollution pose significant threats to their natural habitat.

Cultural and Recreational Value

Beyond their ecological importance, Emerald Gem Clams hold cultural and recreational significance in the Carolinas. They are prized by collectors for their aesthetic appeal and unique coloration, often incorporated into jewelry or displayed as natural art pieces. Beachcombers revel in the thrill of discovering these gems washed ashore, adding to the allure of coastal explorations.

Protection and Preservation Efforts

Local conservation initiatives and regulations are instrumental in safeguarding the habitats of Emerald Gem Clams and other marine species in the Carolinas. Efforts focus on habitat restoration, pollution reduction, and public education to promote sustainable practices among residents and visitors alike.

The Emerald Gem Clam, with its striking beauty and ecological importance, stands as a testament to the natural wonders found along the Carolinas' coastline. As awareness grows about the significance of preserving coastal ecosystems, these enchanting clams serve as ambassadors for marine conservation efforts, inspiring admiration and stewardship among those who encounter them. Whether admired for its aesthetic appeal or studied for its ecological role, the Emerald Gem Clam continues to captivate and enrich our understanding of the diverse marine life inhabiting our coastal waters.

Carolina Marshclam (Polymesoda caroliniana)
The Carolina Marshclam, scientifically known as Polymesoda caroliniana, is a fascinating marine bivalve mollusk found along the coastal regions of the Carolinas, particularly in brackish and freshwater habitats. Known for its distinct appearance and ecological significance, this species stands out among the diverse array of seashells that grace the shores of this region.

Taxonomy and Description

Polymesoda caroliniana belongs to the family Cyrenidae within the order Veneroida. These clams typically grow to a modest size, averaging around 2 to 3 inches in length. Their shells are characterized by a smooth, elongated shape with a glossy surface, often displaying hues ranging from pale beige to light brown. The shells may exhibit subtle patterns or markings, adding to their aesthetic appeal.

Habitat and Distribution

The Carolina Marshclam inhabits estuarine environments where freshwater mixes with seawater, creating brackish conditions that are ideal for its survival. These clams are commonly found buried in sandy or muddy substrates along the shores of tidal creeks, marshes, and shallow coastal waters. Their distribution extends from North Carolina down to South Carolina, where they play a crucial role in the local ecosystem.

Ecological Role

As filter feeders, Carolina Marshclams play a vital ecological role by filtering water and removing organic particles and pollutants, thereby helping to maintain water quality in their habitats. They also serve as an important food source for various aquatic organisms, contributing to the overall biodiversity of the region's estuarine ecosystems.

Cultural and Recreational Significance

Beyond their ecological importance, Carolina Marshclams holds cultural significance in the Carolinas. Historically, Native American tribes utilized these clams as a food source, incorporating them into their diets. Today, they continue to be part of local culinary traditions, prized for their delicate flavor.

For recreational beachcombers and shell enthusiasts, the discovery of a Carolina Marshclam shell is a special find. Its unique shape and subtle coloring make it a sought-after addition to seashell collections. Beachgoers and nature enthusiasts often enjoy exploring tidal flats and estuarine habitats in search of these treasures, adding to the allure of coastal outings.

Conservation Status and Threats

While not currently listed as endangered or threatened, the Carolina Marshclam faces potential risks from habitat loss due to coastal development, water pollution, and climate change. Conservation efforts focus on preserving the quality of estuarine habitats and maintaining sustainable harvesting practices where applicable, ensuring the continued presence of this species in the wild.

The Carolina Marshclam, Polymesoda caroliniana, exemplifies the rich biodiversity and natural beauty of the Carolinas' coastal regions. From its distinctive appearance to its ecological contributions and cultural significance, this humble bivalve mollusk remains a cherished part of the region's natural heritage. Whether admired for its role in the ecosystem, its culinary appeal, or its aesthetic value, the Carolina Marshclam continues to captivate and inspire those who explore the shores and waters of the Carolinas.

Citizen Science and Community Involvement
Collaborative Conservation Projects

The Carolinas, with their expansive coastline along the Atlantic Ocean, boast a rich diversity of marine life, including a fascinating array of seashells. These shells not only serve as natural treasures but also play a crucial role in the ecosystem's balance. To harness community interest and preserve these natural wonders, collaborative conservation projects have emerged, leveraging citizen science and community involvement to protect and study unique seashell finds.

Understanding the Importance of Seashells

Seashells, often found washed ashore, are more than just souvenirs of a beach trip. They provide valuable insights into marine biodiversity, ecological health, and even climate change impacts. Each shell represents a species, habitat, and environmental conditions, making them vital indicators of ecosystem health.

Citizen Science: Empowering Communities to Contribute

Citizen science initiatives in the Carolinas empower residents, schools, and visitors to actively participate in seashell conservation efforts. These projects engage volunteers of all ages and backgrounds, fostering a sense of stewardship and community responsibility toward marine conservation.

Volunteers are encouraged to explore beaches, tidal pools, and coastal areas, documenting seashell species they encounter. Through organized workshops, training sessions, and online platforms, participants learn to identify different shells, record data accurately, and contribute findings to centralized databases. This collaborative approach not only expands scientific knowledge but also enhances public awareness of coastal biodiversity and conservation needs.

Community Involvement: From Education to Advocacy

Beyond data collection, community involvement plays a pivotal role in advocating for seashell conservation. Local organizations partner with schools, museums, and environmental groups to host educational programs and outreach events. These initiatives educate the public about the significance of seashells in marine ecosystems and the threats they face, such as habitat loss and pollution.

Hands-on activities like beach cleanups and habitat restoration projects further strengthen community bonds and promote sustainable practices. By actively participating in these initiatives, residents and visitors alike become ambassadors for coastal conservation, driving positive change through collective action.

Unique Seashell Finds: Inspiring Discovery and Research

The Carolinas' coastal waters are home to a diverse array of seashell species, some of which are rare or unique to the region. Citizen scientists often uncover these treasures during surveys and explorations, sparking interest among researchers and conservationists.

Scientific studies on unique seashell finds help unravel their ecological roles, distribution patterns, and evolutionary histories. By combining local knowledge with scientific expertise, these projects contribute valuable data to ongoing conservation efforts and inform policy decisions aimed at protecting fragile marine habitats.

Preserving Coastal Treasures for Future Generations Collaborative conservation projects driven by citizen science and community involvement are essential for safeguarding the Carolinas' seashell biodiversity. By engaging residents and visitors in hands–on activities, educational initiatives, and research endeavors, these projects foster a deeper appreciation for coastal ecosystems and empower individuals to become stewards of their natural heritage.

Through continued collaboration and advocacy, we can ensure that future generations inherit vibrant and healthy coastal environments, where unique seashell finds continue to inspire awe and scientific discovery. Together, we can make a difference in preserving these precious marine treasures for years to come.

In conclusion, collaborative conservation efforts centered around unique seashell finds in the Carolinas demonstrate the power of community-driven initiatives in protecting and celebrating our natural world.

Educational Outreach Initiatives

The Carolinas, blessed with diverse coastal ecosystems, harbor a wealth of marine life, including an array of unique seashells. These shells not only fascinate beachcombers but also serve as valuable tools for citizen science and community involvement in ecological conservation and education. This article explores the educational outreach initiatives driven by citizen science and community involvement centered around unique seashell finds in the Carolinas.

Citizen Science and Seashell Exploration

Citizen science involves public participation in scientific research, often facilitated by community organizations, educational institutions, and governmental bodies. In the Carolinas, numerous organizations harness the enthusiasm of volunteers to document, study, and conserve unique seashell species found along the Atlantic coast. Volunteers, ranging from amateur enthusiasts to seasoned naturalists, contribute to data collection through organized beach surveys, specimen identification workshops, and ecological monitoring programs.

Community Involvement and Conservation Efforts

Community involvement in seashell exploration goes beyond scientific data collection; it fosters a sense of stewardship and responsibility towards coastal ecosystems. Local communities in the Carolinas actively participate in beach clean-up initiatives that not only remove debris but also safeguard habitats crucial for shell-bearing organisms. Educational workshops and public lectures hosted by marine conservation organizations educate residents and visitors alike about the ecological importance of seashells and their role in coastal biodiversity.

Educational Outreach Initiatives

Seashell Identification Guides and Workshops: Educational institutions collaborate with local natural history museums and environmental nonprofits to develop seashell identification guides tailored to the Carolinas' unique species. Workshops conducted by experts provide hands–on learning opportunities for participants to identify, catalog, and learn about the ecological roles of different seashells.

Interactive Citizen Science Apps: Innovative mobile applications engage citizen scientists in seashell identification and data collection. These apps allow users to photograph and geotag their finds, contributing valuable information to ongoing research projects on shell distribution and abundance.

School Outreach Programs: Elementary and secondary schools' partner with marine biology departments and conservation groups to integrate seashell studies into curricula. Field trips to local beaches and interactive classroom activities deepen students' understanding of marine ecology and conservation principles.

Public Events and Festivals: Annual seashell festivals and public events celebrate the diversity of Carolinian seashells. These gatherings feature expert–led shell walks, art exhibits inspired by marine life, and presentations on current research and conservation efforts.

Impact and Conservation Benefits

The impact of educational outreach initiatives extends beyond academic knowledge to tangible conservation benefits:

Species Conservation: By raising awareness about threatened seashell species and their habitats, outreach efforts contribute to targeted conservation measures.

Public Engagement: Increased public engagement fosters a sense of environmental stewardship, encouraging responsible beach behavior and habitat preservation.

Policy Advocacy: Informed communities are better equipped to advocate for sustainable coastal management policies that protect seashell biodiversity and fragile marine ecosystems.

Educational outreach initiatives by citizen science and community involvement play a pivotal role in enhancing public awareness, fostering community engagement, and promoting the conservation of unique seashell finds in the Carolinas. Through collaborative efforts between scientists, educators, and local communities, these initiatives not only deepen our understanding of marine biodiversity but also inspire a collective commitment to safeguarding our coastal treasures for future generations. As we continue to explore and appreciate the wonders of Carolinian seashells, we pave the way for a more informed and environmentally conscious society.

In summary, the convergence of scientific inquiry, community passion, and educational outreach is shaping a sustainable future where seashell diversity thrives amidst the coastal splendor of the Carolinas.

Map 2: Coastal regions of the Carolinas

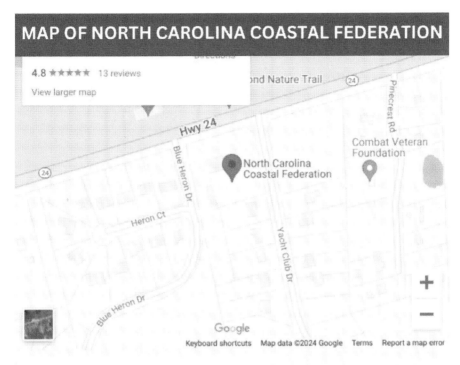

MAP OF NORTH CAROLINA COASTAL FEDERATION

SCAN THE QR CODE

- **Prepare your device:** Ensure your smartphone or tablet has a QR code scanning app installed. Most modern smartphones have built-in QR code readers in their cameras, so you might not need a separate app.

- **Open the QR code scanner:** Launch the QR code scanning app or open your smartphone's camera.

- **Position the QR code:** Hold your device steady and position the QR code within the viewfinder or camera frame. Make sure the QR code is well-lit and not obscured.

- **Scan the QR code:** If you're using a dedicated app, align the QR code within the app's scanning area and it should automatically scan. If you're using your smartphone camera, simply point it at the QR code. Most smartphones will recognize the QR code automatically and provide a notification or a link.

- **Interpret the result:** Once scanned, your device will typically interpret the QR code's data. This could be a URL, text, contact information, or other types of data embedded in the QR code. Follow the prompts on your device to proceed with the information provided.

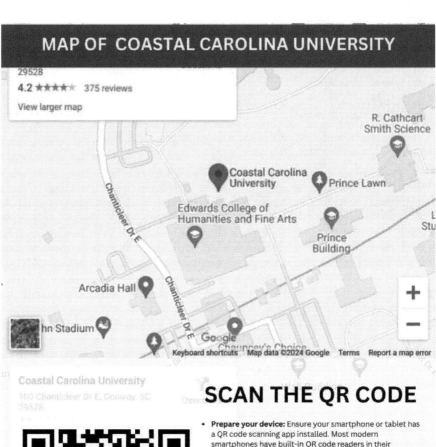

MAP OF COASTAL CAROLINA UNIVERSITY

29528
4.2 ★★★★★ 375 reviews
View larger map

R. Cathcart
Smith Science

Coastal Carolina
University

Prince Lawn

Edwards College of
Humanities and Fine Arts

Prince
Building

Arcadia Hall

hn Stadium

Google

Keyboard shortcuts   Map data ©2024 Google   Terms   Report a map error

Coastal Carolina University
100 Chanticleer Dr E, Conway, SC
29528

SCAN THE QR CODE

- **Prepare your device:** Ensure your smartphone or tablet has a QR code scanning app installed. Most modern smartphones have built-in QR code readers in their cameras, so you might not need a separate app.

- **Open the QR code scanner:** Launch the QR code scanning app or open your smartphone's camera.

- **Position the QR code:** Hold your device steady and position the QR code within the viewfinder or camera frame. Make sure the QR code is well-lit and not obscured.

- **Scan the QR code:** If you're using a dedicated app, align the QR code within the app's scanning area and it should automatically scan. If you're using your smartphone camera, simply point it at the QR code. Most smartphones will recognize the QR code automatically and provide a notification or a link.

- **Interpret the result:** Once scanned, your device will typically interpret the QR code's data. This could be a URL, text, contact information, or other types of data embedded in the QR code. Follow the prompts on your device to proceed with the information provided.

MAP OF COASTAL SOUTH CAROLINA USA

SCAN THE QR CODE

- **Prepare your device:** Ensure your smartphone or tablet has a QR code scanning app installed. Most modern smartphones have built-in QR code readers in their cameras, so you might not need a separate app.

- **Open the QR code scanner:** Launch the QR code scanning app or open your smartphone's camera.

- **Position the QR code:** Hold your device steady and position the QR code within the viewfinder or camera frame. Make sure the QR code is well-lit and not obscured.

- **Scan the QR code:** If you're using a dedicated app, align the QR code within the app's scanning area and it should automatically scan. If you're using your smartphone camera, simply point it at the QR code. Most smartphones will recognize the QR code automatically and provide a notification or a link.

- **Interpret the result:** Once scanned, your device will typically interpret the QR code's data. This could be a URL, text, contact information, or other types of data embedded in the QR code. Follow the prompts on your device to proceed with the information provided.

CHAPTER FOUR

Unique Ways to Make Money from Seashells

Selling Seashells Online: Platforms, Tips, and Market Trends

Exploring the serene beaches of Georgia and the Carolinas can be not only a hobby but also a profitable venture through selling seashells online. Whether you're a seasoned collector or just starting, turning your passion for seashells into a source of income can be both rewarding and enjoyable. Here's a comprehensive guide on how to effectively sell seashells online, including platforms to use, essential tips, and current market trends.

Platforms for Selling Seashells Online

Etsy: Known for handmade and vintage items, Etsy provides a niche market for seashell collectors. Create a visually appealing shop, highlight unique specimens, and write detailed descriptions to attract buyers interested in coastal décor or crafting.

eBay: A global marketplace where you can auction off rare or valuable seashells. Utilize eBay's vast reach to find international buyers who may be seeking specific types of shells from the Southeastern U.S.

Amazon Handmade: Ideal for artisans, Amazon Handmade allows you to showcase your seashell creations alongside other handmade goods. Leverage Amazon's shipping and customer service infrastructure for a seamless selling experience.

Your website: For those serious about building a brand, setting up your e-commerce site gives you complete control over pricing, marketing, and customer relationships. Use platforms like Shopify or WooCommerce for user-friendly setups.

Social media (Instagram, Facebook): Utilize Instagram for its visual appeal by showcasing your seashells in captivating photos. Facebook Marketplace also offers a local selling option, perfect for connecting with buyers in nearby coastal communities.

Tips for Selling Seashells Online

Quality and Authenticity: Ensure your shells are properly cleaned and preserved. Authenticity is crucial; provide accurate information about each specimen, including species, size, and where it was found.

Photography: Invest time in high-quality photography. Natural light and neutral backgrounds can highlight the beauty of each shell. Showcase different angles and close-ups to give potential buyers a comprehensive view.

Detailed Descriptions: Educate buyers about the uniqueness of each shell. Include information on its habitat, rarity, and any special characteristics. Transparency builds trust and enhances the perceived value.

Pricing: Research similar listings to determine competitive pricing. Rare or larger specimens may command higher prices, while common shells should be priced accordingly. Consider offering bundles or themed collections to attract buyers.

Shipping Considerations: Safely package shells to prevent damage during transit. Communicate shipping policies, including costs, handling times, and international shipping options if applicable.

Market Trends in Seashell Selling
Decorative and Crafting Use: Seashells are popular for home décor, crafting projects, and even jewelry making. Capitalize on these trends by showcasing shells that are suitable for these purposes.

Environmental Awareness: Buyers increasingly prefer sustainably sourced shells. Highlight shells collected responsibly, without harm to marine environments, to appeal to eco-conscious consumers.

Local and Regional Appeal: Shells native to Georgia and the Carolinas hold regional appeal. Emphasize the uniqueness of these specimens and their connection to coastal landscapes.

Customization and Personalization: Offer customization options such as drilled holes for jewelry making or personalized displays. This adds value and allows buyers to create unique pieces.

Selling seashells online from Georgia and the Carolinas can be a lucrative endeavor with the right approach. By leveraging suitable platforms, implementing effective selling strategies, and staying informed about market trends, you can turn your passion for seashell collecting into a profitable online business. Embrace creativity, authenticity, and customer engagement to establish a successful presence in the online seashell market. Happy selling!

Crafting and Artisanal Products: Turning Seashells into Marketable Items

Crafting and transforming seashells into marketable items can be both a creatively fulfilling hobby and a profitable venture. Whether you're a beachcomber who loves collecting shells or an artisan looking to explore new mediums, turning seashells into artisanal products can be a rewarding way to make money. Here's a comprehensive guide on how to do just that:

1. Shell Selection and Preparation

Gathering Shells: Start by collecting a variety of shells from the beaches of Georgia and the Carolinas. Look for intact shells with interesting shapes, colors, and textures. Rinse them thoroughly with fresh water to remove any sand, salt, or debris.

Sorting and Cleaning: Sort your shells based on size, type, and condition. Some shells might need gentle cleaning with a soft brush or toothbrush to remove stubborn dirt or organic matter. Ensure they are completely dry before proceeding to the crafting stage.

2. Crafting Ideas and Techniques

Jewelry Making: Seashells can be transformed into stunning jewelry pieces such as necklaces, earrings, bracelets, and rings. Drill small holes carefully using a rotary tool to attach findings or create intricate designs.

Home Decor: Utilize larger shells or shell fragments to craft unique home decor items like wind chimes, candle holders, or picture frames. Combine shells with other natural materials like driftwood or sea glass for added aesthetic appeal.

Artwork and Ornaments: Create shell mosaics on wooden plaques or canvases using strong adhesive. Experiment with arranging shells to form patterns, seascapes, or abstract designs. Paint shells with vibrant colors or metallic finishes for a contemporary twist.

Functional Items: Design practical items such as keychains, coasters, or fridge magnets by embedding small shells in resin or clay. These items are popular as souvenirs or gifts.

3. Enhancing Marketability

Quality and Consistency: Ensure your products are well-crafted with attention to detail. Use high-quality materials for findings and adhesives to ensure durability.

Unique Selling Points: Differentiate your products by incorporating local themes, such as using shells native to Georgia and the Carolinas or incorporating elements from the local culture or environment.

Branding and Packaging: Develop a distinctive brand identity and logo that reflects the coastal inspiration of your products. Use eco-friendly packaging materials to appeal to environmentally-conscious consumers.

Market Research: Attend local craft fairs, farmers' markets, or art exhibitions to gauge interest in your seashell products. Establish an online presence through social media platforms and e-commerce websites to reach a wider audience.

Legal Considerations: Research any permits or regulations regarding the collection and sale of seashells in your area to ensure compliance with local laws.

4. Marketing and Sales Strategies

Photography: Capture high-quality images of your products in natural light to showcase their beauty and craftsmanship. Highlight unique features and textures to attract potential buyers.

Online Platforms: Utilize online marketplaces such as Etsy, Amazon Handmade, or your e-commerce website to sell your products globally. Write compelling product descriptions that highlight the handmade nature and inspiration behind each piece.

Collaborations: Partner with local businesses such as coastal boutiques, gift shops, or tourist attractions to feature your products in their stores or as part of exclusive collections.

Customer Engagement: Engage with your customers through social media by sharing behind-the-scenes content, customer testimonials, or tutorials on shell crafting techniques. Encourage feedback and reviews to build trust and credibility.

5. Scaling Your Business

Production Efficiency: Streamline your crafting process without compromising on quality. Consider outsourcing certain tasks such as packaging or marketing to focus on product development and sales.

Diversification: Expand your product line by incorporating other natural materials or themes inspired by the coastal region. Offer customization options to cater to individual preferences and special occasions.

Learning and Growth: Stay updated with trends in the artisanal market and continue to refine your skills through workshops, online courses, or networking with fellow artisans.

Turning seashells into marketable items requires creativity, dedication, and a keen understanding of your target audience. By leveraging the natural beauty of seashells and your artistic skills, you can create unique products that resonate with customers seeking handmade and environmentally friendly goods.

Educational Workshops and Guided Tours: Sharing Your Passion for Seashells

Creating educational workshops and guided tours focused on seashells in the Georgia and Carolina regions can be a fulfilling endeavor that not only shares your passion but also offers opportunities to generate income. Here's a comprehensive guide on how to effectively monetize and share your knowledge through these activities:

1. Define Your Expertise and Audience

Expertise: Establish your credentials and passion for seashells through years of study, collecting, or personal interest. This credibility will attract enthusiasts and learners alike.

Audience: Identify your target audience, such as families, school groups, amateur collectors, or tourists interested in coastal ecology. Tailor your workshops and tours to meet their interests and knowledge levels.

2. Craft Engaging Workshop Topics

Introduction to Seashells: Start with a foundational workshop covering shell identification, types found in the region, and their ecological significance.

Advanced Identification Techniques: Offer workshops for enthusiasts looking to refine their identification skills using field guides, dichotomous keys, and digital resources.

Seashell Crafts and Art: Include workshops where participants can create jewelry, decorations, or art using shells, appealing to a broader audience interested in crafts.

3. Develop Guided Tour Experiences

Coastal Ecology Tours: Design guided tours along the coastline, explaining the ecosystems where seashells thrive. Discuss conservation efforts and the importance of sustainable collecting practices.

Beachcombing Adventures: Lead tours on local beaches, teaching participants how to find and identify shells. Offer insights into seasonal variations and the best times for shell hunting.

Historical and Cultural Context: Incorporate tours that delve into the historical use of shells by indigenous peoples or their significance in local folklore and traditions.

4. Plan Logistics and Resources

Location Selection: Choose beaches, parks, or nature reserves known for their diverse shell populations and accessibility.

Materials and Tools: Provide participants with necessary tools such as magnifying glasses, field guides, or digital apps for shell identification.

Permits and Permissions: Ensure compliance with local regulations regarding guided tours and any necessary permits for collecting shells or conducting workshops in protected areas.

5. Marketing and Promotion

Online Presence: Create a website or social media profile showcasing your workshops and tours. Share captivating photos of shells and tour activities to attract potential participants.

Collaborations: Partner with local schools, nature centers, or tourist agencies to reach a wider audience.

Offer special rates for group bookings or package deals.

Customer Reviews and Testimonials: Encourage participants to leave reviews and testimonials online to build credibility and attract future customers.

6. Monetization Strategies

Fee-Based Workshops and Tours: Charge a fee per participant for each workshop or guided tour. Consider offering discounts for repeat customers or larger groups.

Merchandise Sales: Sell seashell-themed merchandise such as books, posters, or handcrafted items during workshops and tours.

Private Consultations: Offer personalized consultations for serious collectors or educators looking to deepen their knowledge outside of group settings.

7. Continuous Improvement and Expansion

Feedback Mechanism: Gather feedback from participants to improve the quality of your workshops and tours continually.

Expand Offerings: Introduce seasonal workshops, guest speakers, or themed tours (e.g., night tours for nocturnal shell discoveries) to keep offerings fresh and appealing.

Professional Development: Stay updated on seashell taxonomy, conservation practices, and educational techniques to enhance your credibility and attract a loyal following.

By leveraging your expertise and passion for seashells into educational workshops and guided tours, you not only share your love for these natural treasures but also create a sustainable income stream. Each workshop and tour become an opportunity to educate, inspire, and foster a deeper appreciation for the fascinating world of seashells in the Georgia and Carolina coastal regions.

CONCLUSION

In conclusion, "Seashells of Georgia and the Carolinas: Updated Edition" serves as an indispensable guide and a testament to the enduring fascination of our coastal ecosystems. Through meticulous research and captivating descriptions, this book not only identifies over 200 species of seashells but also deepens our appreciation for the delicate balance of nature.

The authors' dedication to accuracy and detail is evident throughout, making this volume not just a field guide but a gateway to understanding the intricate web of marine life. By emphasizing the ecological significance of each species, the book underscores the interconnectedness of marine habitats and the importance of conservation efforts.

Moreover, "Seashells of Georgia and the Carolinas" is more than a scientific compendium; it is a celebration of biodiversity and a call to action for stewardship. It inspires readers to explore our shores with curiosity and respect, fostering a deeper connection to the natural world.

As we turn the final pages, we are left with a profound sense of wonder at the diversity of seashells and their role in coastal ecosystems. This updated edition not only enriches our knowledge but also encourages us to safeguard these precious habitats for generations to come.

In essence, "Seashells of Georgia and the Carolinas: Update Edition" stands as a beacon of scholarship and passion, inviting us to marvel at the beauty of seashells and to embark on a journey of discovery along our southern shores. It is a reminder that every shell tells a story, and through understanding and conservation, we can preserve these stories for the future.

Made in the USA
Columbia, SC
22 April 2025

fa98234e-c01d-4fd5-9a3c-de792d5e88a5R01